Twins Poems

Compiled by John Foster

Contents

Acknowledgements

The Editor and Publisher wish to thank the following who have kindly given permission for the use of copyright material:

John Foster for Who's who? © John Foster 1991; Roderick Hunt for Biff's poem © Roderick Hunt 1991; Nigel Gray for My twin © Nigel Gray 1991; David Harmer for Which one are you? © David Harmer 1991; Wendy Larmont for Reflections © Wendy Larmont 1991; Robin Mellor for Wish © Robin Mellor 1991; Brian Moses for Twins © Brian Moses 1991; Judith Nicholls for Look-Alike © Judith Nicholls 1991.

Although every effort has been made to contact the owners of copyright material, a few have been impossible to trace, but if they contact the Publisher, correct acknowledgement will be made in future editions.

Printed in Hong Kong

Who's who?

He looks like me.
I look like him.
My name is Zak.
His name is Zim.

Our ears are pointed.
Our fur is blue.
My face is square.
His face is too.

We walk the same.
We talk the same.
The only difference
Is our name.

He looks like me.
I look like him.
Which one is Zak?
Which one is Zim?

John Foster

Which one are you?

Look at me
Look at him
Just the same
Just my twin
Same hair, same eyes
Same face, same size
Same freckles, same nose
Same expression, same clothes.
Same same same!

No I'm not
Nor am I
I'm me
So am I
Different thoughts, different dreams
Different plans, different schemes
Different likes, different hates
Different games, different mates.

Two of us who look the same
But both of us have got a name!

David Harmer

ME
ME

Biff's poem

Same build, same shape,
Same height, same size.
Same light brown hair,
Same hazel eyes.

Yet even though
We're twins, you see,
Chip's not identical
To me.

And when it comes to
How we play,
The way we feel,
The things we say . . .

We're different.

(Oh! And just before
This poem ends . .
We're both the very
Best of friends).

Roderick Hunt

L

(Poem

I'm a . . .
look-alike
hair-alike
play-alike
share-alike

eat-alike
drink-alike
speak-alike
think-alike

sing-alike
scream-alike
laugh-alike
dream-alike

joke-alike
cook-alike
TALK-ALIKE

LOOK

Me too!

Jud

like

in voices)

I'm a . . .
look-alike
hair-alike
play-alike
share-alike

eat-alike
drink-alike
speak-alike
think-alike

sing-alike
scream-alike
laugh-alike
dream-alike

joke-alike
cook-alike
TALK-ALIKE

E TWIN!

Me too!

icholls

Twins

We're hard to pull apart,
we stick to each other like glue
I gave her mumps and measles,
she gave me her dose of the flu.

If she asks to visit the toilet
then I must go there too.
If I can't puzzle out my sums,
she shows me what to do.

If there's a fight I'll protect her,
she does the same for me.
I hold her hand in assembly,
we sing in harmony.

She passes me notes in class
with her name and mine in a heart.
They say we must be twins,
we're never seen apart.

I'm sure there'll never be anyone else
I'd rather have round to play.
If she really were my sister, Mum says,
we'd probably fight all day!

Brian Moses

Wish

I wish I had a Look-Alike
someone who looks like me;
I'd send him to school every day
to do my work for me.

And when Mum calls me in from play,
to wash and go to bed,
Look-Alike could climb the stairs
and go to sleep instead.

Then I could have adventures
out in the park and woods,
and go to bed when I am ready,
just as I think I should.

But if I had a Look-Alike
it could cause a lot of trouble,
birthday gifts and weekend surprises
might be given to my double.

So I'll have to go to school myself,
and come home on time for tea,
I'll have to take the good with the bad
and be glad there's only one me.

Robin Mellor

My twin

My twin does everything I do.
My twin is the mirror image of me:
same face, same hair, same height.

When I wave to him with my right hand,
he waves back with his left.

When I have a graze on my left knee,
he has a graze on his right.

When I speak to him, he speaks to me,
yet says nothing, ever, that I can hear.

And when I rest my hot cheek against his cold one
and breathe on him to try to warm him,
he begins to disappear.

Nigel Gray

Reflections

I look in the mirror
And what do I see?
I see my twin sister.
She's looking at me.

We both look the same
In the clothes that we wear.
The same colour eyes
And the same colour hair.

I look in the mirror
And what do I see?
It's not my twin sister.
I'm looking at me.

Wendy Larmont

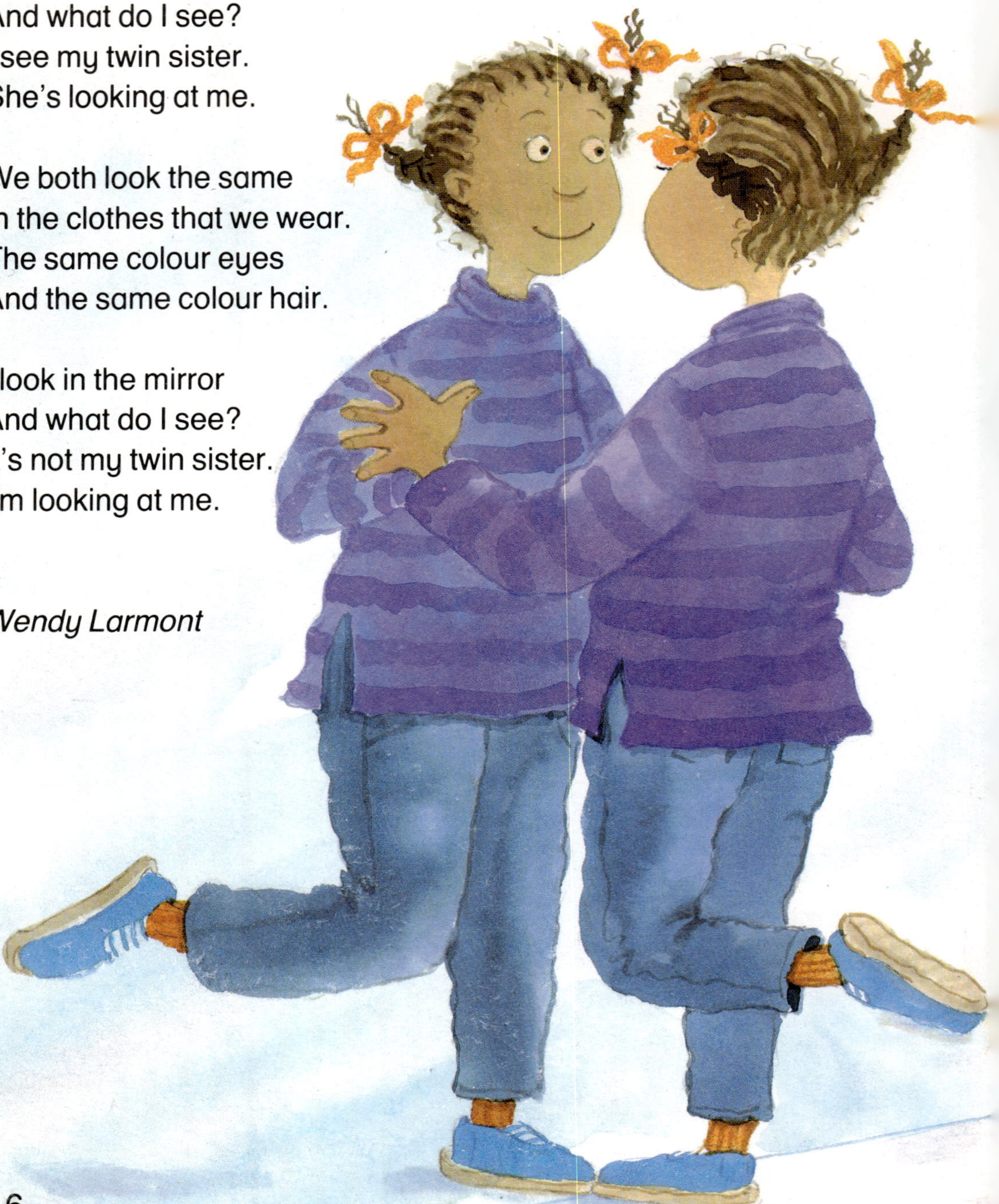